Lorna Doone's Exmoor

A Romantic Picture Guide to the
Land of Lorna Doone

by

Barry Gardner

THE EXMOOR PRESS

4

THE EXMOOR PRESS
Dulverton, Somerset, England

British Library Cataloguing in Publication Data
Gardner, Barry, 1943—
Lorna Doone's Exmoor
1. England. Exmoor—Visitors' guides
I. Title
914.238504859

ISBN 0 900131 66 7

Photographs, Paintings, Illustrations and Maps courtesy of:
Lorna Doone Society
Exmoor National Park
Michael Deering
Bernard Wakeman
Ray Rendell

Front Cover: *The Land of Lorna Doone*
© by Peter Robson

Frontispiece: *Autumn comes to Exmoor*
Back Cover: *East from Foreland*

Printed in Great Britain by Williton Printers, Somerset

Contents

Page

The Land of Lorna Doone 7

The Story of Lorna Doone 13

Eternal Exmoor 23

Lorna Doone's Exmoor...34

The Heart of Dooneland
    The River Lynn...34
    Badgworthy Water..36
    The Waterslide..39
    Doone Valley...40
    The Doone-gate...40
    The Doone-track..42
    Oare Church..43
    Plover's Barrows 44
    Malmsmead 45

The Coast
    Combe Martin..46
    Ley Manor...47
    The Valley of Rocks 49
    Lynton and Lynmouth...49
    Countisbury...52
    Glenthorne..52
    Porlock..54
    Allerford...56
    Dunster..60
    Watchet..60

Around Exmoor...62
    Exebridge 62
    Dulverton...63
    Winsford 64
    Tarr Steps..66
    Landacre Bridge 66
    Exford 67
    Dunkery Beacon..69
    The Wizard's Slough...70

Beyond the Moor...71
    Barnstaple..71
    Molland...72
    North Molton...73
    South Molton...73
    Tiverton 74

Lorna Doone's Exmoor

"As Charles Kingsley
made _Westward Ho!_ part of the National Heritage;
as on a wider and even more durable scale Thomas Hardy re-created Wessex—
so the genius of R. D. Blackmore (flowering, for all his
many other literary labours, in a single novel)
has given Exmoor to the world.

There is plenty of history of all kinds in this delectable region.
The Druids began it and there is many a trace of them still;
but do we think of the Druids today in the Valley of Rocks—or elsewhere?
Old Mother Melldrum, I fancy, is nearer to us still."

Lord Gorell, C.B.E., M.C., 1947.

The Land of Lorna Doone

R. D. Blackmore's Exmoor romance, *Lorna Doone,* first published in 1869, is amongst the foremost of English classics. With much of its content based on fact and folklore, it remains one of the most popular and well-known stories of all time. It is difficult to set foot upon Exmoor without remembering how vividly this wild and magical landscape was portrayed in the headlong narrative of the novel's hero, John Ridd.

Here in this place of ancient barrows and prehistoric stones are beautiful sheltered valleys, sparkling streams and a wealth of wildlife. Nestling amid the hills are some of the most enchanting towns and villages in England.

Selworthy

This is *Lorna Doone Country*—265 square miles of National Park, lying partly in Devon and partly in Somerset, with a boundary of about a hundred miles. Sweeping inland from a majestic coastline, it is a land full of surprises: a wide rolling expanse, with patterned carpets of gorse and heather in a network of babbling water, often giving way quite suddenly to lush pasture, secluded meadows, or perhaps to steep rocky gorges.

The Valley of Rocks

Once a royal hunting ground, the moor is still the home of the wild red deer, the hardy Exmoor pony and the questing buzzard; but among the area's best remembered inhabitants will always be the savage outlaw Doones of the Badgworthy Forest who ravaged the countryside during the 17th century.

The inns and byways of Exmoor were the haunts of the notorious highwayman, Tom Faggus; and the mysterious ground beyond Black Barrow Down hid the secret of Reuben Huckaback's goldmine. Landacre Bridge still holds the gripping memory of the Doone ambush on king's officer Jeremy Stickles; and the commanding height of Dunkery Beacon is an awesome reminder of the vengeful Doone horsemen, as they rode through the fiery storm *"like clouds upon red sunset"*.

These were the days when wheels were hardly seen upon Exmoor. Pony-sleds were mostly used to carry chattels over the rough and marshy terrain, and those who had no horse to ride had to trudge their weary way. There were a few tracks between the major places, trodden by the pack-horses which transported goods across the moor; and numerous little humped bridges were built to take the convoys across the web of streams.

Above:
Robbers Bridge
(between
Porlock and Oare)

Left:
Riders on the summit

Exmoor was perilous for travellers in the 17th century, and there was always the lurking fear of footpads and highwaymen. Smuggling and poaching were rife in the area, and in the mysterious and lonely places were witchcraft and hauntings. But, despite these things, the little towns prospered: Dulverton was a thriving centre of wealth and commerce; Dunster's tannery and cloth trade were widely known, and merchants came from far and near to buy at Porlock Market or at the fishing village of Lynmouth.

Lynmouth

Now there are roads upon the moor, and the once bleak wilderness is an attractive patchwork of well-tended farms and rich grazing land. Gone are the fearsome quagmires and the wayside robbers, and no longer are sheep-stealers to be found hanging at the crossways. But Exmoor is still wild and untamed, for no amount of management and reclamation has diminished the attraction of the heath-clad hills, the bright singing waters, or the deep winding valleys. The dawns and sunsets are as magical as ever; and the quaint old villages, with their thatched roofs and historic churches, are still reminiscent of Doone times, as they snuggle quietly in the comfort of overhanging woods, or beneath the steep cliffs by the coast.

Left:
An Exmoor Pony

Rarely has any author so immortalised or popularised an area as did R. D. Blackmore in *Lorna Doone,* and the novel's romantic pages contain the finest and most detailed descriptions of Exmoor ever written.

"All by the hedge ran a little stream . . . flowing scarce more than a pint a minute, because of the sunny weather. Along and down the tiny banks, and nodding to one another . . . hung the brown arcade of ferns . . . fanning over with the grace of yielding, even as a hollow fountain spread by winds that have lost their way. God has made no finer thing, and only He takes heed of them."

Below:
Oare Water
(The Lynn Stream)

The Story of Lorna Doone

'A Romance of Exmoor' by R. D. Blackmore

The tale is set in the turbulent reigns of Charles II and James II, when Exmoor was terrorised by the marauding Doones—a high-born family outlawed from their native Scotland because of a feud over land with the Earl of Lorne.

In or about 1640, the exiled Sir Ensor Doone and his followers settled, destitute, deep in an Exmoor combe, not far from the parish of OARE and, here in this sheltered and naturally fortified place, the outlaws built their own settlement of fourteen cottages. The stronghold was so formidable, and the outlaws were so feared, that no man would dare venture anywhere near the DOONE VALLEY.

As the years passed, the Doones became ever more notorious, and they cared little for the lives or property of their neighbours. Robbery and murder were commonplace to them, as were firing houses and plundering crops. They even carried off the farmers' daughters to be their wives.

Opposite:
Woody Bay

Below:
In the heart of
Doone Country

On his birthday in November 1673, young John Ridd of Oare was brought home from BLUNDELL'S SCHOOL in Tiverton, following his father's murder by Carver Doone, the most fearsome of the outlaws. John was only twelve years old, but the time had come for him to take up his duties with his mother and sisters at their PLOVER'S BARROWS FARM.

John was collected from Blundell's by the Ridd's farmhand, John Fry, and on their journey they stopped to dine at DULVERTON, where they saw a fine lady and her children who were travelling in a coach bound for WATCHET. John could not help but notice the young daughter and her beautiful long dark hair; but the travellers went their separate ways, and John thought little more about her.

On St. Valentine's Day, a little over two years later, John Ridd went fishing for loaches in the RIVER LYNN, near his home. Having no success, he decided to explore along the wild BADGWORTHY WATER, which took him into the land of the Doones, and to the foot of a rushing WATERSLIDE. He climbed to its top and fell asleep on the grass.

"If you please, my name is Lorna Doone" (Brock)

He was woken by a lovely young girl, who wondered if John might be lost, for no-one ever came on purpose to the Doone Valley. It was the girl from the coach at Dulverton, and she told him she was Lorna, the granddaughter of the outlaw captain, Sir Ensor Doone. John could not help liking her, even though she was a Doone, tainted by his father's murder; and the memory of that meeting stayed with him for the seven years till he ventured to see her again.

John was twenty-one when he next met Lorna at Glen Doone. She had become a most beautiful young lady, and John fell in love with her. But the wise woman of Exmoor, Mother Melldrum, who lived at THE VALLEY OF ROCKS, warned him not to pursue his dangerous acquaintance with the outlaw maid, for nothing but harm would come of it.

"Lorna led me into her little bower" (Brock)

In spite of the warning, they did continue to see each other, and John learned that Lorna was held almost as a prisoner by her own family. She had no friends but John, and was not allowed beyond the valley. Worse still, she was betrothed to Carver Doone—the very man who had killed John's father!

John, who had grown to great size and strength, vowed that he would face the wrath of Carver and rescue Lorna but, quite unexpectedly, he was called away to London. A king's officer named Jeremy Stickles arrived at Plover's Barrows, with a summons for John to appear before the Court of His Majesty's Bench at Westminster.

At the Court, John was confronted by the infamous Judge Jeffreys, who wanted to know all about the Doones. There were plots against the Crown brewing in the West Country, and Jeffreys thought the outlaws might be involved. He also quizzed John about the Exmoor Baron De Whichehalse of LYNTON who, it was suspected, was in league with the Doones.

Towards
Lee Bay
— near Lynton

On returning to Oare, John learned that he was not the only member of his family to fall in love with an outlaw. His sister Annie confided that she had been meeting secretly with their cousin Tom Faggus, a highwayman from NORTH MOLTON. Tom was a popular and jovial fellow who had been a renowned blacksmith, until ruined in an unjust law-suit by a jealous nobleman. Following this calamity, he had taken to the road and gained a great reputation as a champion of the poor.

Left:
In Badgworthy Wood

Below:
Weir Water Valley

John had not dared tell his mother about Lorna, but he knew he must do so at once for, if Lorna was to be saved from Carver Doone, she must be brought out of the valley to live with the Ridds at Plover's Barrows. John also feared that it would not be long before Jeremy Stickles led a military assault against the Doone stronghold, having been commissioned by Judge Jeffreys to forestall a local rebellion.

In the Doone Valley, Sir Ensor Doone was dying; Carver would become the new captain and Lorna's fate would be sealed. In desperation, Lorna told Sir Ensor about her love for John Ridd, who was called before the old Doone.

Sir Ensor had no wish for Lorna to marry Carver. He was content to give his blessing to John, although quick to point out that Carver would seek revenge, and John's life would be in danger. Then the old man gave Lorna an ancient necklace, familiar from her childhood. On the next day he was dead.

John managed to rescue Lorna from the Doone Valley, under cover of a mighty blizzard and the greatest frost of the century. Taking advantage of the cold, he pulled Lorna down the frozen Waterslide on a roped sled, while the Doones were celebrating Carver's new captaincy by the firelight from DUNKERY BEACON.

Winter comes
to Exmoor

Oare in the Valley

Lorna settled in quickly at the farm. To her surprise, she learned from Jeremy and Tom that her old necklace was not glass as she thought. It was made of diamonds, and its clasp bore a noble crest. But, Carver Doone knew this. He lurked nearby—swearing revenge on the Ridds and recapture for Lorna. His father, The Counsellor, took the first step and stole the necklace from Plover's Barrows.

While investigating threats to the Crown, Jeremy Stickles was ambushed by the Doones at LANDACRE BRIDGE. Luckily he escaped with his life, and told John Ridd what he had discovered: Lorna was not a Doone at all, and the diamonds were her true family heirloom. She had been kidnapped by the outlaws from her mother's coach at Watchet, on the very day that John had seen her those many years before. Lorna was not Sir Ensor's granddaughter, but the daughter of the Doones' Scottish enemy, the Lord Dugal, and descended from the ancient lords of Lorne. Carver meant to marry Lorna when she came of age, and so claim title to her lands and inheritance—giving the Doones a foothold again in Scotland.

There was no time to lose, and Jeremy Stickles prepared an attack on the Doone stronghold. But, instead of the troopers which had been promised, he had to use the local militia who were quite untrained and no match for their fierce adversaries. While John and Jeremy led an assault against the DOONE-GATE at the main entrance to the outlaws' valley, the militia fired from the hills. It ended in disaster, with the militia fighting each other, and the Doones won the day.

Soon afterwards, Lorna was summoned to take up her rightful position, as Lady Lorna Dugal, at the royal palace in London. John was very distressed to see her go, but the Doones and other matters kept him well occupied. His great-uncle, Reuben Huckaback, a wealthy clothier from Dulverton, was greatly worrying the family with his insistence that he had found a gold-mine on the moor—deep below the great black swamp of THE WIZARD'S SLOUGH.

By this time, Annie had married Tom Faggus and gone to live at MOLLAND but, after the death of King Charles, Tom had left to join the Duke of Monmouth's rebels who were mustering against the new King James. At Annie's request, John went in search of Tom but, by the time he arrived at Sedgemoor, the battle had been fought and won by the king's men. Many of the rebels had been slain, and others were to face Judge Jeffreys at the assizes. Even John was taken for a rebel, seized by the soldiers, and was lucky to escape hanging by the timely arrival of Jeremy Stickles, who had him released. Meanwhile, the wily Tom Faggus escaped, safe and sound.

"Stout ropes were
flung about me"
(Brock)

Eventually, John followed his beloved Lorna to London, with little hope that he, a common yeoman, would be allowed to resume his friendship with a lady of the Court. Happily, his fears were quite unfounded: the king knighted him for his bravery, and Lorna's guardian, the Earl Brandir of Lochawe, even gave consent to their marriage.

And so, Sir John Ridd and Lady Lorna Dugal returned to Exmoor where their wedding was duly arranged. But in John's absence the Doones had committed a hideous kidnapping and murder. So, before his marriage, John resolved to lead a great army of outraged countrymen in one last desperate attack on the Doone Valley. This time the Doones were defeated, every one of the outlaws' homes was burned to the ground, and The Counsellor was forced to return Lorna's diamonds. Carver Doone alone escaped.

In Oare Church

The great day of the wedding at OARE CHURCH came. John and Lorna stood to receive the parson's blessing. A shot rang out and Lorna fell upon the altar steps. Carver Doone had taken his revenge.

"Carver felt his
time had come"
(Brock)

John chased Carver on horseback across Black Barrow Down to
the Wizard's Slough, where they fought hand-to-hand. The
advantage moved from one to the other. In the struggle, neither
noticed that they were moving ever closer to the edge of the terrible
quagmire. Suddenly, Carver's feet were caught in the deep heaving
mud. John lost his hold, and the vicious Carver Doone sank out of
sight to his death.

John returned to the church to find Lorna still alive—she had only
been wounded by Carver's bullet. At last, the Doone reign of terror
was over for ever, and Lorna and John lived happily at Plover's
Barrows.

Eternal Exmoor

The Exmoor known by the Doones existed over 300 years ago. Therefore much that can be seen now would not have been witnessed by Lorna herself. Nevertheless, by the 1600s the moor already had a long and exciting history, during which the desolate wastes of prehistoric times had been much altered by the hand of man. In the succeeding centuries the landscape has matured and been developed further into the beautiful panorama of today.

The Early Years

It is thought that Exmoor was inhabited as long ago as the early Stone Age; there are certainly traces of Neolithic life in the area. A wealth of evidence, however, comes from the Bronze Age (c. 2000-500B.C.)—not the least of which are the numerous chieftains' burial mounds *(barrows)* and the many stone monuments including the mysterious 9½-foot *Longstone* near Chapman Barrows.

During the Iron Age, waves of Celtic invaders from the Continent reached the moor. Tension ran high between these intruders and the native inhabitants who sought to protect themselves with fortified earthworks *(castles)* on high ground. The new settlers, in turn, were forced to construct similar defences in the face of attack from later Celtic colonizers, and the remains of their hill-forts can still be seen at such commanding sites as Countisbury and Shoulsbarrow.

The Romans

Subsequently, about the year A.D. 48, the Romans came to Exmoor but, for the most part, their occupation was confined to the brief operation of two coastal stations at Old Barrow and Martinhoe. Otherwise, it appears that the moorland people were left to themselves in their bleak surroundings, although Latin inscriptions on some standing-stones imply that they absorbed an element of Roman culture.

Once the Romans had withdrawn from Britain in A.D. 410, and the shadow of the Dark Ages had fallen, Exmoor—like the rest of the country—was a target for invasion. Saxon penetration of the West Country was a slow process, particularly when the Britons were led by the legendary King Arthur. For all that, by around 700 the Saxon occupation of Exmoor was complete.

The Caratacus Stone on Winsford Hill (inscribed in the Dark Ages)

The Saxons

For over 300 years the Saxons were masters of the moor, naming such places as Oare *(Are)* and Badgworthy *(Baga Wordia)*. Their rule was not unchallenged and, in the 9th and 10th centuries, Vikings menaced the coast. However, their raids on Exmoor were successfully repulsed, notably at Watchet and Porlock, which was far from the case in other parts of the country.

The Saxon era—the age of the great kings of England such as Alfred and Edward the Confessor—was a time of great development on the once primitive moor. Land was organised into a series of manors and farms, whilst the uncultivated waste came to be regarded as the property of the king. All of this is well described in the Domesday Book of 1086.

The Royal Forest

In 1066 England fell to the Norman conquerers under Duke William. As King William I, he kept the Saxon settlement structure, but replaced the Saxon lords with Norman knights as land-barons on Exmoor. Dunster went to William de Mohun, and Porlock to Baldwin of Exeter. Robert d'Obdurville was appointed as the first Warden of Exmoor, and the deer were preserved for the pleasure of the king. Thus the centre of the moor became a Royal Forest *("Forest" meaning an unenclosed area of land—in this case used as a royal hunting ground)*, and was retained for the monarch's use throughout the Norman and Plantagenet periods. Indeed, there were some very peculiar ground-rules laid for those residing in this kingly domain: Walter of Oare, for example, was only allowed to hold land by virtue of his providing Edward I with hunting arrows.

Red-deer stag

In 1508, the Tudor King Henry VII introduced a system of *leasing* the Royal Forest to its Warden, in return for an annual payment which the Warden more than recouped by charging for grazing rights on the moor. And later, in commemoration of his first marriage, Henry VIII settled Exmoor upon Catherine of Aragon.

Following the execution of King Charles I in 1649, much Crown land was sold off to private individuals. The Exmoor Forest was purchased in 1652 by James Boevey—a London merchant of Dutch origin—who became the most notorious Warden of the moor, which he ruled from his purpose-built lodge at Simonsbath. He was a most unpopular fellow who laid claim to lands outside his purlieu, and started numerous legal actions against his neighbours.

After the Restoration of Charles II and the Stuart Monarchy in 1660, earlier Crown property, including Exmoor, reverted to the king but, despite the attempted intervention of the royalist Marquis of Ormonde, Boevey managed to retain the Exmoor Forest leasehold, and stayed on as Warden until his death in 1696.

Above:
Boevey's Simonsbath House

Opposite Above:
Dunster Castle

Opposite Below:
The remote Stoke Pero Church (recorded in the Domesday Book)

The method of leasing the Forest to subsequent Wardens continued throughout the following century. The last of the Wardens was Sir Thomas Dyke Acland, whose application for renewal of the lease in 1814 was declined. This was the time of the Napoleonic Wars, and it was decided that part of Exmoor should be maintained for Naval oak production, with the rest parcelled out to interested landholders, including Sir Thomas Acland and Sir Charles Bampfylde. After the battle of Waterloo, however, the need for timber diminished and the Government resolved to sell its allotment outright. It was purchased by John Knight, an iron-master from the Midlands. By 1820, John Knight and his son Frederic had bought out Acland, Bampfylde and other landowners, to possess two-thirds of what had been the Crown's Exmoor lands. The age of the Royal Forest was over.

Sheep on Exmoor

Reclamation and a New Era

During the 19th century, the Knights probably did more than anyone before to get the best out of the moor. Their objective was reclamation and, at no little cost to themselves, they financed building projects; improved and constructed roads; worked mines, and introduced new farming methods, so that towards the end of the century Exmoor was a truly flourishing place.

Sadly, Frederic Knight's only son died young and, without an heir, Frederic determined to sell. In 1897 the Knight estate passed to the Fortescue family, who already owned much land in the area and, in turn, they sold some of the joint-holding to Sir Robert Waley Cohen in 1927. After the Second World War, other portions were sold to outside purchasers.

Following the National Parks Act 1949, it was decided that, although mostly privately owned, Exmoor's beauty and wildlife deserved protection, and the moor was proclaimed a National Park in 1954. Now the heritage of Exmoor is preserved in a setting that defies comparison anywhere in England.

Overleaf:
An Exmoor
Farmstead

Below:
Exmoor House —
headquarters of the
National Park
Dulverton

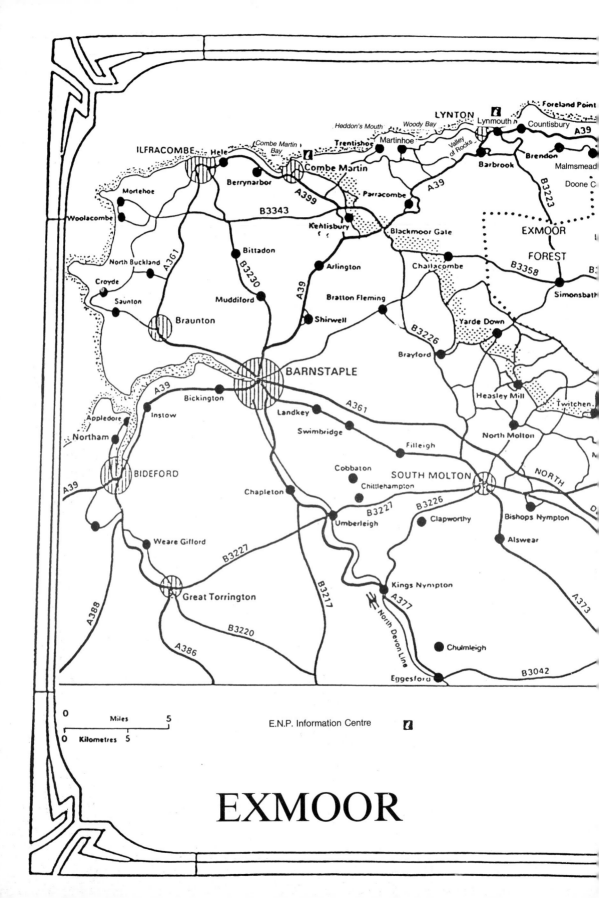

EXMOOR

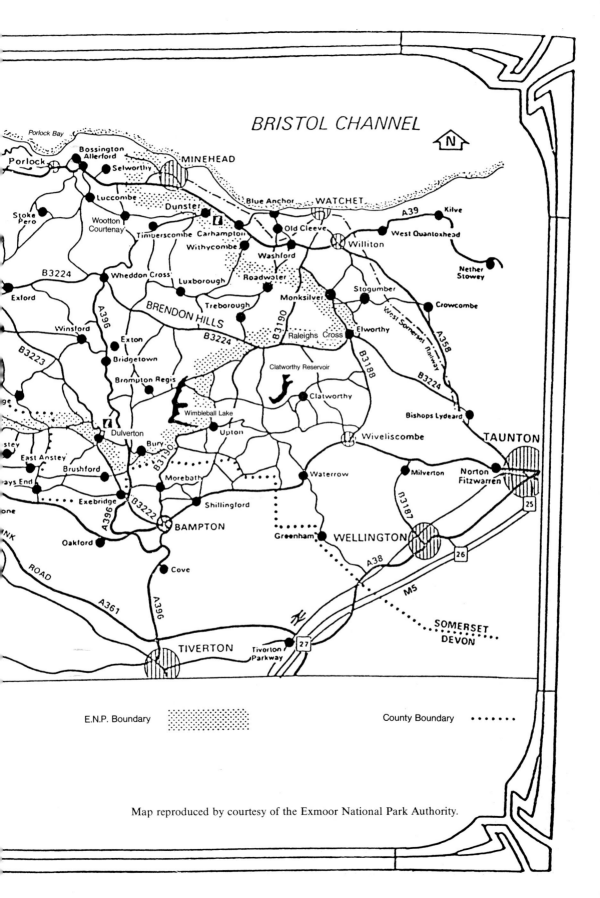

BRISTOL CHANNEL

Map reproduced by courtesy of the Exmoor National Park Authority.

E.N.P. Boundary ⋯⋯ County Boundary ⋯⋯

Lorna Doone's Exmoor

The Heart of Dooneland

River Lynn

"But all below, where the valley bends, and the Lynn stream goes along with it, pretty meadows slope their breast, and the sun spreads on the water, and nearly all of this is ours."—L.D. Chap. 7.

John Ridd's much loved fishing ground, the River Lynn, was a marriage of the East Lyn River and Oare Water *(which he called the Lynn stream)*. The name Lyn *(or Lynn)* comes from the Saxon, *hlynna (torrent)*, and the river's pools and reaches have long been the haunt of fishermen who explore for trout and salmon; although the loaches, which John describes in *Lorna Doone,* have long since disappeared.

The East Lyn, near Brendon

"But when I was down on Saturday the thirteenth of June, at the blacksmith's forge by Brendon town, where the Lynn stream runs so close that he dips his horse-shoes in it, and where the news is apt to come first of all our neighbourhood . . . came a man on a pie-bald horse . . ."—L.D. Chap. 62.

The prattling waters of Oare to which John refers are, however, only the beginning of the Lyn's story, for it is a river of many personalities—running gently at first through tree-clad Brendon pasture, and becoming ever wider and more resolute as it prepares to surge deep into the valley.

The old parish of Brendon includes remnants of the estates of Lank Combe and Badgworthy, which were listed in the Domesday Book, and which are very relevant to the story of *Lorna Doone.*

Near Watersmeet

"Thence it hurries away with strength and a force of wilful waters, under the foot of a bare-faced hill, and so to rocks and woods again, where the stream is covered over, and dark heavy pools delay it."—L.D. Chap. 7.

The East Lyn is noted for the numerous deep pools which steady its flow as it crashes over countless rocks and ledges in the formidable sheer-sided valley beyond Brendon. At length, the river is swelled by the swirling torrents of Farley and Hoaroak, which provide a glorious sight at Watersmeet. And further down the gorge the West Lyn adds its strength to the flow, which finally surrenders to the sea at Lynmouth.

Badgworthy Water

"Now all the turn of my life hung upon that moment . . . It seemed a sad business to go back now . . . and yet it was a frightful thing, knowing what I did of it, to venture where no grown man durst, up the Bagworthy Water."—L.D. Chap. 7.

John Ridd's fear of the Bagworthy *(now Badgworthy—pronounced Badgery)* was not for the water itself. Indeed it is a most appealing little river, which glides northwards to unite with Oare Water and form the East Lyn at Malmsmead. Doubtless its banks were more densely wooded in the 1600s, but John's real dread of this waterway was that it fed from the Doone Valley.

Badgworthy Water

"I found it strongly overwoven, turned and torn with thicket-wood, but not so rocky as the Lynn, and more inclined to go evenly."— L.D. Chap. 7.

The Badgworthy is a favourite with dippers and kingfishers, and its course forms part of the Devon-Somerset border. On its bank, across from Cloud Farm, is a memorial stone erected to R. D. Blackmore, whose writings in *Lorna Doone* gave such recognition to this enchanting place.

The Blackmore
Memorial

In Saxon times there was a farm estate at Badgworthy *(Baga's Manor)*, and by the 12th century this settlement was held by the Brethren of the Hospital of St. John of Jerusalem. The hamlet, at the lower end of Hoccombe Combe, continued in use through Norman times, and until the reign of Henry IV. The village then fell into decay, and there is no record of any habitation from the middle 1400s, except for an old fellow and his daughter who camped among the ruins in the early 19th century.

In about 1860, many of the stones from the ancient houses were used to build a shepherd's hut nearby—which was very convenient for some eager guide-book writers who later claimed that this was Lorna Doone's cottage, and further attributed the medieval ruins to the homes built by the Doones in the 17th century! Fortunately, and for security reasons, this latter-day shepherd's hut was blown up by the Army during the Second World War. Now there are but a few ground-level remains of the ancient hamlet to be seen.

It is clear from the records of Buckland Abbey that the early village of Badgworthy supported a resident priest, and the building remnants certainly indicate that there was a chapel. Indeed, it was here in the derelict *"little chapel-yard"* at Hoccombe that Sir Ensor Doone is said to have been buried—*"three miles to the westward of the Wizard's Slough"*.

38

The Waterslide

"For lo! I stood at the foot of a long pale slide of water, coming smoothly to me . . ." LD. Chap. 7.

So begins young John Ridd's introduction to the notorious Doone Valley — The famous *Waterslide* which he climbed on St. Valentine's day 1675-6. Having struggled barefoot to its top, he fell onto the grass and was later awakened by the lovely Lorna Doone.

The Waterslide became John's favoured route into Glen Doone where he met with Lorna in her secret bower. And as he grew in stature, his boyhood memory of the awesome ascent lessened somewhat into an adult reality of the more accommodating waterway which he encountered again in mild weather.

"And still the great rocky slide was dark, and difficult to climb; though the water, which had once taken my knees, was satisfied now with my ankles." LD. Chap. 16.

Following the death of Sir Ensor Doone, and in the grip of a terrible winter, John used the frozen slope as Lorna's escape-route from the Doone encampment — guiding her down the shining iceway on a roped sled.

"All my waterslide was not less a slide than a path of ice . . . how it was easy track and channel, as if for the very purpose made, down which I could guide my sledge, with Lorna sitting in it." LD. Chap. 44.

Fortunately for those on the Lorna Doone trail, there has never been any doubt as to which waterslide Blackmore referred in *Lorna Doone,* for in 1882 he commissioned his own painting of the *Doone Valley Waterslide* — the waterslide of Lank Combe.

John Ridd's Waterslide entrance to the Doone Valley is there today — complete with its dark whirling pool when the stream is swollen — running out of Lank Combe, 1¾ miles from Malmsmead along the Badgworthy Water. Earlier this century, the northern bank of the slide was cut away to facilitate an easier path for visitors — and a little wooden foot-bridge has been placed at the foot of it. But the southern side is still steep and rocky, as it would have been in Doone times.

Opposite:
The Waterslide

Doone Valley

"She stood at the head of a deep green valley, carved from the mountains in a perfect oval . . ." LD. Chap. 4.

At the head of the Waterslide lies the Doone Valley of *Lorna Doone* — more generally known as Lank Combe. The hills, which rise to over three-hundred feet above the combe, overlook an oval landscape, wherein the little river runs like a street through the valley.

"I marked the position of the houses . . . the stream, in lieu of any street, passing between . . ." LD. Chap. 37.

". . . the captain's house was a sort of double-house . . . joined by a plank over the river." LD. Chap. 4.

Here in this defendable place, the Doones built their single-storey huts in the Scottish croft tradition — mostly of timber framework, filled with stones and peat, under roofing of turf and moss.

". . . The house was of one storey only, as the others were, with pine ends standing forth from the stone . . . The Doones had been their own builders, for no-one should know their ins and outs . . ." LD. Chap. 37.

From their self-built stronghold, the Doones terrorised the neighbourhood for many decades during the 17th century, until the country-folk at last took revenge and burned the outlaws' settlement to the ground.

"And the earliest notice The Counsellor had, or anyone else, of our presence, was the blazing log-wood house, where lived that villain Carver . . . And of all the dwellings of the Doones . . . not even one was left, but all made potash in the river." LD. Chap. 71.

The Doone Valley can be reached by following the track from Malmsmead along the Badgworthy Water and up the path before the Waterslide footbridge.

The Doone-gate

"The journey was a great deal longer to fetch around the Southern hills, and enter (the Doone Valley) by the Doone-gate, than to cross the lower land, and steal in by the waterslide . . . the rocky mouth was spanned, as by a gallery, with brushwood and piled timber, all upon a ledge of stone . . ." LD. Chap. 37.

John Ridd describes that at the head of the Doone Valley *(the opposite end to the Waterslide)* was the main entrance to the outlaws' settlement — the *Doone-gate.*

"In the early afternoon she came to a hollow and barren entrance, where in truth there was no gate." LD. Chap. 4.

The principal entrance to the stronghold was not a gate as such, but a fortified archway of felled trees, supported upon a rock formation to form a gallery which could be guarded by sentries. The large supportive rock still stands at the high end of Lank Combe.

Above:
The Doone Valley

Left:
Doone-gate rock

The Doone-track

"Hould thee tongue lad," he said sharply. "Us be naigh the Doone-track now . . ." LD. Chap. 3.

The Doone-track is often referred to by Blackmore as a robbers' highway which ran across the moor to the Doone-gate. No mention is ever made of the outlaws entering Glen Doone by the Waterslide route or from the Badgworthy Water end.

The route is impossible to plot in its entirety, since many moorland tracks have changed or been obliterated over the years. We do know, however, from Blackmore's descriptions, that it led out of the high western end of Doone Valley, and then swung around to traverse eastwards across the moor to the north of Chibbet Post, somewhere near Alderman's Barrow — where the track was crossed by John Ridd and John Fry — and towards Dunkery Hill where the Doones would fire the beacon to light their journey.

The Doone-track

Oare Church

"So we buried him quietly — in the sloping little churchyard of Oare, as meek as a place needs be, with the Lynn brook down below it." LD. Chap. 5.

The Church of St. Mary the Virgin has been the parish church of Oare for more than eight-hundred years, and the font-basin dates back to the 12th century. Oare Church has gained international fame as the place where Lorna was shot and wounded by Carver Doone on the day of her wedding to John Ridd.

Oare Church

The nave and present inner chancel are externally much as they would have been in the Doone era — still with 15th century roofing, although the interior was restored in Georgian times. However, the church was much smaller when Lorna and John were married, for the eastern chancel is a 19th century addition. Therefore, the altar steps where Lorna fell would have been set further back to the west of the present screen.

". . . a shot rang through the church and those eyes were dim with death. Lorna fell across my knees . . . and a flow of blood came out upon the yellow wood of the altar steps." LD. Chap. 74.

Blackmore makes no mention of the shot coming from anywhere in particular — only that it *"rang through the church"*. However, the interpretation of a 1920's silent film gave rise to a now popular tradition that Carver fired through a side-window. More probably the shot would have come down the nave from the western end.

Oare House —
Plover's Barrows site
from the church

Plover's Barrows

"Almost everybody, in our part of the world at least, knows how pleasant and soft the fall of land is around Plover's Barrows farm. All above it is strong dark mountain spread with heath and desolate, but near our house the valleys cove and open warmth and shelter. Here are trees, and bright green grass, and orchards full of contentment, and a man may scarce espy the brook, although he hears it everywhere." LD. Chap. 7.

John Ridd's home, Plover's Barrows, shown on tithe maps as the Oare Farm, stood on the site now occupied by Oare House. The old farmhouse was demolished in 1883, but much of the original stone, including the fireplace wall, was used for the new building, and some of the earlier outbuildings still exist today.

Shortly before Blackmore's death, flowers from Oare Farm were sent to him in recognition of the place he had immortalised so vividly in *Lorna Doone.*

The site provides an excellent view of Oare Church, as John Ridd so aptly describes when his sister Annie watched her father's funeral from the window of the house; or as John Fry explains in relation to his young master's gun-siting. Indeed, it is still the only house in the vicinity which gives a direct gun-barrel view of the church-yard, as described.

"Maister Jan, thee can see the grave (from Plover's Barrows) if thee look alang this here goon-barryel." LD. Chap. 6.

Malmsmead

Malmsmead

"In the evening, Farmer Snowe came up (to Plover's Barrows), leading his daughters after him like fillies trimmed for a fair." LD. Chap. 14.

Malmsmead — known in the 18th century as *Moles Mead* — is a truly delightful setting, where the Badgworthy Water is prettily bridged by a ford and near to the old Malmsmead farmhouse. The house was renamed Lorna Doone Farm in the early 1900s as a part of the local tourism enterprise, and a gift-shop was subsequently introduced in view of the increasing popularity of the area.

Down the hill from Oare Church, this farmhouse — the western part of which is a thousand years old — has little to do with Lorna herself, nor is Malmsmead in the Doone Valley as is claimed by some tour operators. However, the building was very relevant to John Ridd's narrative, since this was the home of the Snow family until the Oare Manor House became theirs by marriage in the 18th century.

Oare records show that a Snow daughter was married from this farmhouse in 1699. Therefore, Blackmore was correct to include the family in his account of things, along with the fact that their land bordered on the lower part of Plover's Barrows.

"But all below (Plover's Barrows) where the valley bends, and the Lynn stream goes along with it, pretty meadows slope their breast, and the sun spreads on the water. And nearly all of this is ours, till you come to Nicholas Snowe's land." LD. Chap. 7.

The Coast

Combe Martin

"I thought at once of the tales I had heard concerning mines at Cornwall, and the silver cup at Combe Martin sent to the Queen Elizabeth." LD. Chap. 58.

Combe Martin was named after Martin de Tours — one of William the Conqueror's lieutenants (as also was Martinhoe).

This seaside village, on the north-western fringe of the National Park, has a long straggling street of nearly two miles in length, and was famous for its silver production from the 13th century until 1875. The mining wealth helped to pay for the French wars in the reigns of Edward III and Henry V. A new vein was discovered in 1937, but the mines are now all closed and have ceased to operate.

The impressive headlands of Great Hangman and Little Hangman may be reached by a steep climb from Combe Martin.

Combe Martin

Ley Manor

"When we arrived at Ley Manor, we were shown very civilly into the hall, and refreshed with good ale . . . I have never been under so fine a roof. I had seen the Baron De Whichehalse before, and was not afraid of him . . . because we knew his house was in decadence."
LD Chap. 15.

The home of the Baron de Whichehalse was the old Manor at Ley, where Lee Abbey now stands on the coast near Lynton.

Lee Abbey

In the middle 16th century a Nicholas Wichehalse was Mayor of Barnstaple, and the family were noted wool-merchants. Following the Barnstaple plague in 1646, Hugh Wichehalse took up permanent residence at the family's Ley Manor, becoming Squire in the area. He was a very popular and well respected gentleman to whose memory a plaque was erected in Lynton Church in 1653. However, following his death, the Wichehalse finances fell into decline, and by 1676 the family purse was practically empty. Because of heavy mortgage debts, Hugh's son John Wichehalse was forced to sell off the Manor estate.

In 1640, R. D. Blackmore's ancestor, Richard Blackmore of Parracombe, married Margaret Wichehalse of Ley; and it was Ursula Babb, the granddaughter of Wichehalse servants, who provided some of the material for the earliest writings about the exploits of the outlaw Doones — long before Blackmore took up his pen on the subject. Indeed, it was Ursula's grandfather who assisted Squire Wichehalse in the capture of Major Nathaniel Wade at Farley, after the Battle of Sedgemoor.

The present Lee Abbey was built on the old Manor site in 1850 and, whilst never an abbey, it is now used as a Christian residential centre.

Right:
The Devil's
Cheesewring

Below:
Lynmouth Harbour

The Valley of Rocks

"Now Mother Melldrum kept her winter in this Vale of Rocks, sheltering from the wind and rain within the Devil's Cheese-ring." LD. Chap. 17.

The wise woman's winter abode was high in an unusual cliff-top vale near Lynton. This picturesque and rugged part of the North Devon coast, with some of the highest cliffs in England, is a product of the Ice Age and frequented by goats.

The Valley of Rocks runs, unusually, parallel to the sea, and it is thought to have carried the Lyn river many thousands of years ago. It has sometimes been called the Valley of Stones and, in the 18th century, was referred to as The Denes.

The Devil's Cheese-ring *(Cheesewring)* is explained by John Ridd as *"a queer old pile of rocks",* set behind the great Castle Rock, from where there are magnificent views of The Bristol Channel. The Cheesewring is so called because of its likeness to a giant cheese-press. Other prominent rocks in the valley are Ragged Jack and The White Lady.

Lynton and Lynmouth

"We knew for certain . . . there was much disaffection towards the King . . . especially when we heard of arms being landed at Lynmouth, in the dead of night, and of the tramp of men having reached someone's ears . . ." LD. Chap. 32.

The twin towns of Lynton and Lynmouth are set splendidly in the rugged cliffs of the North Devon coast — one high and the other low — to provide a perfect combination of chough's nest panorama and quayside charm.

Lynmouth, traditionally a fishing village, sits at the mouth of the East and West Lyn rivers — and 500 feet above is the largely Victorian Lynton.

Lynmouth displays the harbour and parkland, whilst Lynton boasts magnificent views of Countisbury and The Foreland. Westwards of Lynton is the romantic Valley of Rocks and the picturesque Lee and Woody Bays.

The towns are linked by a steep road, and also by a unique 900-foot cliff railway, which was built in 1890. The track climbs a 1:1¾ gradient and the two cars are gravity-driven by means of complementary water-tanks.

Right:
North Walk, Lynton

Near Lynmouth is the wonderland of Watersmeet, where the Hoaroak and Farley Waters cascade into the East Lyn. It was from here in 1952 that devastating floods fell upon the town. Following an unusually wet period, the night of 15th August saw a final catastrophic rainfall, and the high Chains area could soak up no more. The rivers swelled and flooded — gaining momentum as they drove into the rocky gorges from which there was no escape, except to the sea. Hoaroak, Farley and the West Lyn joined forces with the East Lyn — bringing trees and boulders along with the raging torrent which ravaged little Lynmouth, causing great loss of life and property.

Subsequently, engineers have taken extensive precautionary measures, and have redesigned the water-courses to prevent such a destructive occurrence in the future.

Lynton and Lynmouth have now, visually at least, recovered from their wounds and their combined attraction is such that they are a great favourite with tourists and holidaymakers, who know the area affectionately as *England's Little Switzerland.*

Opposite:
The Glen Lyn Gorge

There is an Exmoor National Park Information Centre at Lynmouth.

Countisbury

"Knowing how fierceley the floods were out, I resolved to travel the higher road by Cosgate and through Countisbury . . . I could see all the inland valley ribbon'd with broad waters; and in every windy crook the banks of snow that fed them, while on my right the turbid sea was flaked with April showers." LD. Chap. 48.

Countisbury is a very small hamlet, comprising only a few cottages, an inn, and a church which was built in two stages — 1796 and 1835.

The main historic feature is the hilltop fortress — an Iron Age earthwork known as Countisbury Castle and, from a thousand feet above sea-level, there are splendid views of the Welsh coast.

Cosgate, to which John Ridd refers, is County-Gate where Exmoor National Park have another Information Centre. Once there actually was a gate here across the highway to separate Devon and Somerset.

Opposite Above:
The coast
by Glenthorne

Glenthorne

"How the year went by I know not, only that I was abroad all day shooting, or fishing . . . or away by the seaside below Glenthorne, wondering at the great waters, and resolving to go for a sailor." LD. Chap. 9.

Like much of Exmoor, the Glenthorne estate is private property, but the waymarked tracks allow wonderful views of some of the finest coastal scenery in England.

The house at Glenthorne sits like an eagle, looking out above a hundred-and-fifty foot drop to the sea. But there is another farmhouse nearby, which readers of *Lorna Doone* will remember well:

". . . happening to fire the ricks of a lonely farmhouse called Yeanworthy, not far above Glenthorne, they (the Doones) approached the house to get the people's goods, and to enjoy their terror. The master of the house was lately dead, and had left . . . loaded, the great long-gun . . . Now Widow Fisher took out this gun . . . upon which she pulled the trigger with all the force of her thumb . . ." LD. Chap. 48.

Not many people got the better of the fearsome Doones, but the widow of Yenworthy was certainly an exception — with a dead outlaw to her credit after this escapade. It was said that, afterwards, the robbers asked of the lady's age, and said that *"She ought to be a Doone!"*

Opposite Below:
Yenworthy

Porlock

"I saw only sheep and small red cattle, until I was nigh to Porlock town, and then rode straight to Mr. Pooke's at the sign of the Spit and Gridiron." LD. Chap. 6.

This fascinating village, nestling at the foot of the notorious Porlock Hill (the steepest main-road hill in the country) is recorded from Saxon times.

Old Porlock

It was once a land-locked port, and for many centuries had its own harbour where the Danes landed in the 10th century. But later the sea withdrew and the separate Porlock Weir developed, leaving Porlock village marooned two miles inland.

The oldest part of St. Dubricius Church dates back to the 13th century, and it was named after the reputed Celtic missionary who was said to have solemnised the marriage of King Arthur and Guinevere. There are many charming tales as to the reason for the unusually truncated wooden spire, but it was in fact damaged by a storm in 1702.

Here in this place of cottages famed for their tall chimneys and back-to-front aspect *(Porlock-style)*, sat the druggist's premises of Master Pooke, where John Ridd purchased two great packages of gunpowder and a mighty chunk of lead, for a shilling. John also had his Will made in Porlock, by as honest a lawyer as he could find!

Porlock Weir

At the foot of Porlock Hill stands the thatched Ship Inn, reputed to have been used by Coleridge and Southey; and this may well be where John Ridd's father took his ease before setting homewards on his last fateful day.

"My dear father had been killed by the Doones of Bagworthy, while riding home from Porlock market, on the Saturday evening . . . a man, beyond the range of staff, was crouching by the peat-stack, with a long gun set to his shoulder, and he got poor father against the sky." LD. Chap. 4.

It is traditionally supposed that the killing of John's father took place in the region of Robbers Bridge, on the road from Porlock to Oare. However, the bridge itself was not built until long after Doone times — there being only a ford across the river in the 17th century.

Near to Porlock, high in the coastal woods, is the tiny parish church of Culbone — measuring internally only 12 feet wide and 12 yards long. In olden days the surrounding woods were inhabited by lepers and charcoal burners.

Eighty-six of Lord Harrington's archers and twenty-eight lancers were trained at Porlock, before fighting in France after the Battle of Agincourt in the early 15th century.

Allerford

"Mr. Reuben Huckaback . . . owned the very best shop in town (Dulverton) and did a fine trade in software, especially when the pack-horses came softly in at Christmas time." LD. Chap. 13.

Apart from the coaches which used to transport people between some of the larger towns, the use of the wheel came very lately to Exmoor, and most of the farmers used pony-sleds to convey their materials over the rugged moorland.

For centuries though, the main method for transportation of merchandise in the area were the sturdy pack-horses, and these were a common sight to see, trekking overland and often in convoy, weighed down with fleeces and all manner of goods going out of Exmoor; and other requirements coming in.

The moor is webbed with streams and little rivers — therefore, to accommodate the important pack-horses, special narrow humped bridges were built in any number of convenient places. One of the prettiest of these is remarkably preserved at Allerford, near to the picturesque villages of Selworthy and Bossington.

The Pack-horse Bridge at Allerford

The quaint tall-chimneyed Bossington, set close to Hurlstone Point, is famed for its walnut trees. And Selworthy, on the former Acland estate, is the epitome of English rural perfection, with its thatched, dormer-windowed cottages and carefully tended green.

Bossington

Allerford sits in the Porlock Vale, at the foot of the Selworthy and Bossington Beacons — from where the views of Exmoor and the Bristol Channel are breathtaking.

Overleaf:
Porlock Vale

Dunster

*"Now I never saw a prettier town than Dunster looked that evening
. . . I had almost lost hope of reaching it that night, although the castle
was long in view . . ."* LD. Chap. 27.

Dunster is indeed one of Exmoor's most fascinating and most
popular villages, with fine examples of old English architecture. The
magnificent castle which crowns the scene was heavily restored in
Victorian times, but was first built for William de Mohun in 1080.
Now open to the public and owned by The National Trust, the castle
was the home of the Luttrells for 600 years from 1376 when they
bought it for £3,400.

Situated in the attractive cobble-paved High Street can be seen the
octagonal Yarn Market, built in about 1609 when Dunster had a
thriving cloth trade; and the ivy-clad Luttrell Arms dates back to
1443. It was originally a residence for the Abbots of Cleeve, but by
1651 had become an inn trading at the sign of The Ship. The present
name was adopted in 1779 from the Luttrell Lords of the Manor.

Dunster also boasts a medieval dovecot which housed two-
thousand birds; an operative water-mill; a 14th century monks' house
(renamed The Nunnery in 1769); the impressive 15th century St.
George's Church with its 100-foot tower; a doll museum, and the
remains of the medieval Butter Cross from where butter was sold
when it stood in the High Street many centuries ago.

Dunster is now a flourishing tourist resort, with an Exmoor
National Park Information Centre, but still retains the unique charm
that John Ridd would have known so well. However, in John's era,
and until the 18th century, there was an additional row of buildings,
known as The Shambles, which ran down the centre of town.

Opposite Above:
Dunster

Watchet

*". . . I hastened to Watchet the following morning, before the sun
was up . . . and so, without interruption, I was in the churchyard at
sunrise."* LD. Chap. 57.

Although outside of Exmoor, Watchet is of course very relevant to
Lorna's story, for it was here that she was kidnapped by the outlaw
Doones whilst travelling in the coach with her mother, the Countess
Dugal, and her nurse, Benita.

The 12th century church of St. Decuman's (the parish church of
Watchet) was where John Ridd sought to find the unmarked grave of
Lorna's mother, who had been buried there — far away from her
native Scotland, following her tragic assault by the Doones.

St. Decumanus was a famous Celtic missionary, and the church is
said to be built on the site where he was murdered in the
7th century.

Opposite Below:
St. Decuman's,
Watchet

Around Exmoor

Exebridge

"Dear Tom (Faggus) knew much of the world . . . and could have thrown light upon Lorna's history if we had seen fit to apply to him . . . He had stopped her mother's coach . . . on the Bampton road, the day before I saw them." LD. Chap. 60.

Young Lorna and her mother would doubtless have passed over the fine old stone Exe Bridge on their coach ride from Bampton to Dulverton — before Lorna ever dreamed of The Doone Valley, her future husband John Ridd, or any of the story that was to follow.

The beautiful River Exe is, of course, the christening water of Exmoor — born high in The Chains, and near to 30 feet across as she flows under the proud archways by The Anchor Inn, on the site where the elusive highwayman Tom Faggus was ultimately captured by the constables.

Here, at Exebridge, on the southern fringe of the National Park, is where Lorna first entered the enchanted domain which was to forge her legend and become her home.

Exebridge

Dulverton

"It was high noon before we got to Dulverton that day, near to which town the River Exe and its big brother Barle have union. My mother had an uncle living there, but we were not to visit him that time. But now at Dulverton we dined on the rarest and choicest victuals that I ever did taste." LD. Chap. 3.

The Barle at Dulverton

In Doone times, the old town of Dulverton had many more taverns than it has today, but Blackmore does not name the hostel to which John Ridd and John Fry came on that sad day in November 1673, after young John's father had been murdered by the Doones. Nevertheless, their *"hot mooton pasties — dished up in the tin with gravy",* must be one of the best remembered meals ever set into print.

John's great-uncle Reuben Huckaback, a worthy clothier and said to be the richest man around, lived at Dulverton with a house at the top of the town, and a profitable shop also at the sign of The Gartered Kitten. Jury Road has been claimed as a likely place for Reuben's residence; however the shop (now Doone House) was in Fore Street. The original premises were burned out in 1922, and are now replaced by a supermarket store.

Once a great hunting town with a monthly cattle auction, Dulverton was certainly a busy place — its industry powered by water from the shining River Barle. Indeed, it was at Dulverton that Alfred Lord Tennyson wrote of Exmoor as *"the land of bubbling streams".* Today, at the southern gateway to Exmoor, Dulverton remains a thriving rural centre and a fitting home for the Exmoor National Park Authority.

A life-sized bronze of young Lorna Doone — commissioned by Dr. Whitman Pearson of New England, U.S.A. — is being placed by Exmoor House, Dulverton, suitably near to where John Ridd first laid eyes on his future bride as she travelled in the coach with her mother, the Countess Dugal. The statue was sculpted by Prof. George Stephenson at Exeter, and was donated to the town by Dr. Pearson in 1990.

Opposite:
Winsford

Winsford

"But though I may have been none the wiser for my stay in London, at any rate I was much the better in virtue of my coming home again. For now I had learned the joy of quiet . . . and running waters and the sounds of country life . . ." LD. Chap. 28.

The little village of Winsford is the personification of John Ridd's sentiments; for here is the feel of country life and the tranquillity of running waters which he could never forsake for the city.

Crowned by its fine old church, which displays the Arms of James I, Winsford is one of Exmoor's most attractive villages, where numerous tiny bridges cross the River Exe and its capricious tributaries as they trickle about the town.

The politician, Ernest Bevin, was born at Winsford; and the nearby Winsford Hill (owned by the National Trust) is a favourite spot for birdwatchers and naturalists.

Tarr Steps

"Mother Melldrum had two homes . . . In summer she lived in a pleasant cave . . . close to Tarr Steps . . ." LD. Chap. 17.

This ancient clapper bridge, where the wise woman had her summer home, spans the River Barle at Hawkridge, a little way from Dulverton. It is indeed one of the wonders of Exmoor, and might be anything up to 3,000 years old. Some maintain that the bridge is medieval, but the name is presumed to derive from the Celtic, *Tochar* (causeway), therefore the Steps could have their origins in the Iron Age.

The causeway consists of seventeen spans of dry-stone slabs, weighing up to two tons each, and the Steps are supported about three feet above normal water level for 120 feet — with a total length of about 180 feet.

John Ridd has it that Tarr Steps were built by Satan for a wager! But whatever the age or origin, this mighty work is surely a phenomenon of early engineering.

Tarr Steps

Landacre Bridge

"All the way from Landacre Bridge, I have ridden a race for my precious life . . . three great Doones galloping after me."
LD. Chap. 47.

The exciting Doone ambush of king's officer, Jeremy Stickles, was at Landacre Bridge (pronounced *Lanakker*), which crosses the River Barle near Withypool. At over 400 years old, it is one of the longest-standing stone bridges in England, and is shown on 17th century maps as Long Acre Bridge.

Landacre Bridge

Exford

"I wore over to Exford in the marning", John (Fry) began . . . "as I coom down the hill, I zeed a saight of volkes astapping of the roudwai . . . they was arl gooin' to be promoted for kitching of Tom Faggus."
LD. Chap. 39.

This parish village on the River Exe and central to the moor, is the prominent stag-hunting centre, with its busy inns and hill-top church.

Exford was the scene of one of Tom Faggus's most daring adventures, when he actually joined forces with a party of men who were sent to apprehend him. Being unrecognised, he suggested to them that, since the weather was damp, they should all fire their guns in the air to check the priming. This they duly did, except for Tom, who then robbed the men at the muzzle of his own gun and, before they had time to reload, he announced himself and rode away unharmed.

Dunkery Beacon

"For now the beacon was rushing up in a fiery storm to heaven . . . the flinging fire leaped into the rocky mouth of the glen below me, where the horsemen passed in silence . . . like clouds upon red sunset . . ." LD. Chap. 3.

Opposite:
Exford

Dunkery Beacon, which the Doones fired to light their way homewards upon the Doone-track, was set at 1705 feet — the highest point on Exmoor, and the site provides magnificent views over more than a hundred miles of countryside.

Below:
Dunkery skyline

Between the 14th and 17th centuries, Dunkery's rocky height was a signal station, and one of a series of fires used to announce the coming of the Spanish Amada. Now a cairn of stones marks the beacon spot — but bonfires were lit there once again in 1969 to commemorate the centenary of *Lorna Doone's* publication.

The Wizard's Slough

"Therefore John (Fry) rode down the slope with sorrow . . . suddenly he turned a corner and saw a scene which stopped him . For there was the Wizard's Slough itself, as black as death and bubbling . . ." — LD. Chap. 31.

The fearful black swamp where the Ridd's farmhand, John Fry, thought he saw a man rise from the marsh; and where the savage Carver Doone met his end, does not exist today as portrayed by Blackmore. The most dangerous area now is The Chains, high on the moor near Brendon Two-gates — a desolate and wet plateau at an altitude of 1,500 feet. Nevertheless, in 1689 Exmoor was more generally recorded as being *"a very barren place, and very full of bogges."*

"The black bog had him (Carver Doone) by the feet; the sucking of the ground drew on him, like the thirsty lips of death . . . Scarcely could I turn away, while, joint by joint, he sank from sight." — LD. Chap. 74.

Blackmore describes the terrible quagmire as being across Black Barrow Down from Oare, and a good ride north-east of the Exford road in a direction towards Cloven Rocks.

Other directional indicators are that the Slough was well to the east of The Warren, and three miles eastwards of the little Hoccombe chapel-yard. The area plotted by these descriptions is still shown on large-scale Ordnance Survey maps as *Black Mires*, near to Alderman's Barrow.

John Ridd's eccentric uncle, Reuben Huckaback, mined for gold beneath the Wizard's Slough; and it is clear that mines have long existed on the moor. Iron, copper, tin and manganese, have all been operated. Also there are records of searches for silver and gold in the locality.

The bleak Wizard's Slough area

Beyond The Moor

Barnstaple

"As for poor Tom Faggus . . . being caught upon Barnstaple Bridge with soldiers at either end of it (yet doubtful about approaching him), he set his strawberry mare, sweet Winnie, at the left hand parapet . . . without a moment's doubt she leaped it into the foaming tide." — LD. Chap. 75.

Such is the tale of Tom Faggus's most dramatic escape from justice — a forty-foot death-defying flight on his enchanted horse.

Barnstaple, on the River Taw to the west of Exmoor, is North Devon's most prominent town, and has a thousand year-old Charter (one of the oldest in the land).

In earlier times the town had a series of iron gates at its entrances, and these were closed at night to keep out tramps and unwanted travellers.

Barnstaple was the home of a great shipping industry, and five of the town's ships joined Drake's fleet at Plymouth, to meet and defeat the Spanish Armada in 1588. This significant trading centre was ravaged by plague in 1646, as was Bideford. Today, however, the town has a bustling shopping centre, and the Guidhall houses a magnificent silver-plate collection.

Barnstaple Bridge

Molland

"Tom Faggus had very good news to tell . . . he had taken up his purchase from old Sir Roger Bassett of a nice bit of land, to the south of the moors, and in the parish of Molland." LD. Chap. 46.

In the 16th and 17th centuries many influential Devonshire families had farms and property around Molland. It was here, to the east of North Molton and on the margin of the National Park, that John Ridd's sister Annie went to live after her marriage to Tom Faggus. Molland has a 15th century church with a well preserved Georgian interior — and the reckless parson of 1803 was Blackmore's inspiration for the nefarious Parson Chowne in his novel, *The Maid of Sker.*

Molland

North Molton

"By trade he (Tom Faggus) had been a blacksmith, in the town of Northmolton, in Devon, a rough rude place at the edge of Exmoor . . ." —LD. Chap. 12.

Beyond the lower Exmoor boundary is North Molton, once the domain of the powerful land-owning Bampfyldes. Here Tom Faggus lived and had his blacksmith's forge, before he fell foul of an unjust lawsuit and subsequently became a renowned and popular highwayman.

Tom's place of business stood close to the Poltimore Arms — where the Courts Leet and Baron *(feudal tribunals)* were held. The Faggus smithy was demolished in 1896.

South Molton

"But I happened to have a little flat bottle of the best stoneware slung beneath my saddle-cloak, and filled with the best 'eau de vie', from the George Hotel at Southmolton." — LD. Chap. 47.

South Molton

As the name implies, below North Molton lies its larger neighbour, South Molton (once nicknamed *Gossip-town),* still with the George Hotel, and with its handsome parish church whose churchyard saw one of the final skirmishes of the Civil War.

Tiverton

"My father being of good substance ... sent me his only son to be schooled in Tiverton in the county of Devon. For the chief boast of that ancient town (next to its woollen-staple) is a worthy grammar-school, the largest in the West of England, founded and handsomely endowed in the year 1604, by Master Peter Blundell ..."
— LD. Chap. 1.

South of Exmoor lies Tiverton, where young John Ridd was educated at the famous Peter Blundell's School. Indeed, this was R. D. Blackmore's own school from 1837 to 1843.

The triangular patch of turf between the causeway, called the *Ironing-box* (where John Ridd fought with Robin Snell), and Old Cop's arched gateway are still to be seen, although in John Ridd's day the gates were wooden — the iron replacements not being fitted until 1695.

Old Blundell's

In 1882 a new school was built about a mile away, and the old Jacobean building, on the bank of the Lowman River, now belongs to The National Trust.

Near to Old Blundell's, in Gold Street, is the grey-stone chapel gateway and the historic 15th century Greenway Almshouses — opposite to which stands the White Horse Inn, where twelve-year-old John Ridd stayed on the night of his leaving school.

"We left the town of the two fords . . . after lying one day to rest, as was demanded by the nags . . . and we lodged at the sign of the White Horse Inn, in the street called Gold Street, opposite where the souls are of John and Joan Greenway . . ." — LD. Chap. 3.

Also at Tiverton, perched above the River Exe, is the Castle, commissioned as a royal fortress by King Henry I. It was later defortified after the Stuart Restoration, and largely rebuilt as a grand residence. Nevertheless, the 12th–17th century buildings are in remarkable condition, and house an impressive Civil War armoury.

Having now journeyed beyond Exmoor to Tiverton, we have returned to where John Ridd's famous adventure began more than three-hundred years ago. Behind us now lies Oare Church, Black Barrow Down and the Wizard's Slough—still alive with their memories of outlaws and rebellion. This was the inspired scene for one of the greatest love stories ever told. This is The Land of Lorna Doone.

Selected Reading List

First Published		Author	Publisher
1869	*Lorna Doone*	R. D. Blackmore	Sampson Low
1893	*Annals of the Royal Forest of Exmoor*	Edwin J. Rawle	Barnicott & Pearce
1900	*Reminiscences of a West Country Clergyman*	Rev. W. H. Thornton	Iredale
1901	*A Short History of The Original Doones of Exmoor*	Ida M. Browne	Cox Sons
1901	*The History of Part of West Somerset*	C. Chadwyck-Healey	Sotheran
1903	*The Doones of Exmoor*	Edwin J. Rawle	Barnicott & Pearce
1903	*A Book of Exmoor*	F. J. Snell	Methuen
1906	*The Blackmore Country*	F. J. Snell	A. & C. Black
1907	*The History of Lynton & Countisbury*	Rev. J. F. Chanter	Commin
1909	*The Somerset Coast*	C. G. Harper	Chapman & Hall
1925	*The Land of Lorna Doone*	H. Snowden Ward	Sampson Low
1925	*The Lorna Doone Country*	Alfred Vowles	Sampson Low
1926	*Exmoor Memories*	A. G. Bradley	Methuen
1929	*Doone Valley & The Waterslide*	Alfred Vowles	Western Gazette
1930	*Richard Doddridge Blackmore*	J. Quincy Burris	Univ. of Illinois
1930	*Wild Exmoor through the Year*	E. W. Hendy	Cape
1939	*The Story of the Doones*	L. B. Thornycroft	Barnicott & Pearce
1944	*Blackmore & Lorna Doone*	T. Warnock Smith	Brodies
1947	*Lorna Doone Country*	S. W. Colyer	Ward Lock
1953	*The North Devon Coast*	S. H. Burton	Werner Laurie
1953	*Exmoor*	L. Meynell	Robert Hale
1956	*R. D. Blackmore*	Prof. Waldo H. Dunn	Robert Hale
1956	*Exmoor Wanderings*	Eric Delderfield	E. R. D. Publications
1960	*The Last Victorian*	Rev. Kenneth Budd	Centaur Press
1966	*Waymarked Walks — Exmoor*		Exmoor National Park
1968	*The Facts on which Blackmore based Lorna Doone*	Sir Athol Oakeley, Bt.	The Author
1969	*Journal of the Blackmore Society*		Blackmore Society
1970	*Ships and Harbours of Exmoor*	Grahame Farr	Exmoor Press
1970	*Portrait of Exmoor*	J. H. B. Peel	Robert Hale
1970	*The Reclamation of Exmoor Forest*	Orwin & Sellick	David & Charles
1972	*The Exmoor Handbook*	N. V. Allen	Exmoor Press
1973	*The History of the Forest of Exmoor*	E. T. MacDermot	David & Charles
1974	*Churches and Chapels of Exmoor*	N. V. Allen	Exmoor Press
1975	*The Lorna Doone Trail*	S. H. Burton	Exmoor Press
1978	*The Waters of Exmoor*	N. V. Allen	Exmoor Press
1978	*Exmoor*	S. H. Burton	Robert Hale
1980	*The Hostage Heiress of Doone Valley*	Dr. Whitman Pearson	The Author, U.S.A.
1981	*In Quest of the Doones*	A. Elliott-Cannon	Breakaway Books
1983	*Ancient Exmoor*	H. Eardley-Wilmot	Exmoor Press
1984	*Exmoor Villages*	Berta Lawrence	Exmoor Press
1985	*Enjoying Exmoor*		Exmoor National Park
1985	*Secret Exmoor*	Peter Hesp	Exmoor National Park
1987	*Exmoor National Park*	Dr. Glyn Court	Webb & Bower
1989	*Who Was Lorna Doone?*	Barry Gardner	Brendon Arts